How Time Has Weathered Me

WalkerDoodle Press

Also by Art Elser

We Leave the Safety of the Sea

A Death at Tollgate Creek

As the Crow Flies

To See a World in a Grain of Sand

It Seemed Innocent Enough

A High Plains Year in Haiku

It Begins in Silence, Ends in Grace

Memoir

What's It All About, Alfie?

How Time Has Weathered Me

Poems

Art Elser

WalkerDoodle Press

Copyright © 2024 Art Elser
All rights reserved.

No part of this book may be reproduced or transmitted in any form or by any means, electronic or mechanical, including photocopying, recording, or by any information storage and retrieval system without the expressed written permission of the author, except in the case of brief quotations in critical articles and reviews.

ISBN-978-1-7366449-0-4

WalkerDoodle Press
Denver, CO 80220

As Always for Kate
The Love of My Life

Contents

Crows Begin and End Each Day 1
Gazing into Star-filled Space on a Summer Night 2
This Beautiful, Wild Creature 3
What Noise in the Ancient Silence 4
With Snow in Tomorrow's Forecast 5
A Belted Kingfisher 6
The Roan Colt Chases His Shadow 7
Dueling Pronghorns on a Fall Morning 8
A Red Fox Family Meal 9
Best Not to Get Rattled 10
A Small Black Spider Visits 11
Our Small Hummingbird Feeder 12
The Ancient Peach Blooms Again 13
Mother and Toddler in the Coffee Shop 14
Hope Is the Thing With feathers 15
An If-only Moment 16
The Sick Child 17
My Biennial Echocardiogram 18
A Poem That Doesn't Want To Be Written 19
Backyard Sounds 20
First Love Remembered 21
Lament of the Jilted #2 Dixon Ticonderoga 22
An Old Typewriter's Memories... 23
The Moon by Earthlight 24

A Brief Scent of Rain	25
The Winter Solstice	26
A Spring Afternoon in January	27
The Backyard on a Cold January Day	28
A Sunday Afternoon in Early March	29
Warming in the Early Spring Sun	30
Spring Dawn at Monte Vista	31
A Bluebird Morning on the Prairie	32
A Summer Morning's Gift	33
Swallowtail	34
A Good Summer in the Rear View Mirror	35
As Summer Ends	36
The Wildlife Refuge Eases into Fall	37
A Walk on an Indian Summer Day	38
A Trip to the Prairie to Enjoy Its Fall Colors	40
Collapsed Barn	42
As I Walk Through Aztec Ruins	43
The Ancient Call of Sandhill Cranes	44
A Day Along the Rio Grande	46
Growing up on Long Island	47
My Disastrous First Day in First Grade	48
Grade School in a Small Village	49
The Steaming Manure Pile	50
The Slow Crawl of Time	51
My Childhood Memories Are Rare	52

A Little Night Music	53
They Called Me the Big Rock	55
Karl's Old McCormick Deering Tractor	56
A Small Green Studebaker	58
First Flight	59
Kill Devil Hill, December 17, 1903	60
Learning to Spin the T-37	61
North of Greenville, MS, July, 1960	62
One Dark October Night, 1962	63
Flying As a Gift, a New Way of Seeing	64
Flying Gliders from a Grass Field	65
Consider the Wind	66
Birth of a Thunderstorm	67
I Ride the Wind	68
How I Miss My Flying Days	69
Memoir	71
A Quiet Morning Over Vietnam	72
English 405, Grad School, May 1970	73
After the Interview	74
Mom's Old Peach Tree	75
My Mother-in-Law, My Mom	76
My Sense of Time Has Changed	77
Letter to a Woman I Met at a Writing Workshop	78
How Time Has Weathered Me	79
At the Cardio Rehab Center	80

I Want My Forty-year-old Body Back	81
I Try to Calculate my Net Worth	82
Faces from the Long-Ago Past	83
About the Author	84

One sees clearly only with the heart
Anything essential is invisible to the eyes.

> Said by the fox in *The Little Prince*
> by Antoine de Saint-Exupery

Crows Begin and End Each Day

Each day flights of noisy crows
fly east through the growing dawn
from their local communal roosts.
It's as if they call to wake the sun
and help it climb into the day.

Small groups feed on grass seeds
in road medians, elbowing out
small gaggles of Canada geese.
It is January and there are crows
like black flowers on the snow.

In the evening, as the day falls
behind snow-topped mountains
and darkness rises in the east,
the crows fly west silently back
to their communal roosts.

        Lines in italic from Mary Oliver's "Crows"

Gazing into Star-filled Space on a Summer Night

> *. . . to read the long lines*
> *of cold code written in the stars*
> *"Tomorrow," Barbara Crooker*

As I lay in the grass at night at the Great Sand Dunes, enchanted by the star-glutted night overhead, I wonder not only how many billions of stars, but how many billions of galaxies I see, each with its billions of stars. And this but a small piece of the entire universe.

I can't help thinking there could be thousands of small forgettable planets with civilizations, each an experiment by some god to see which survives to become the model for new civilizations that love and respect their planet, ones which find creative ways of caring for their legacy.

And as that god has seen our bent to destroy humankind and other life forms on this spaceship we share, it has turned away, paying no more attention to us than a cat to a dead mouse. That god has left us alone to extirpate ourselves or change how we live and save our planet.

This Beautiful, Wild Creature

The August sun is low in a cloudless lupine sky
and wonderfully hot on my body. I've climbed
to this hideaway of boulders above a dirt road,
to sun bathe, buck naked, at a workweek's end.

I munched the peanut butter and jelly sandwich
I brought from home and now sip a cold beer
as I enjoy the peace and solitude, sun's warmth
and quiet that radiates from the large boulders.

Suddenly a thin coyote appears on a game trail
that crosses just below an opening in the rocks.
I couldn't see her until she got to that opening.
She stops, startled, looks at me, seems confused.

As she realizes I'm a human, her eyes show fear.
She's frozen there watching me. I am also startled,
but when I see her fear, I speak very softly to her
to let her know that I mean her no harm.

She understands, relaxes, trots slowly away.
I lean back against a warm rock, filled with joy
and wonder, amazed by what just transpired
between me and this beautiful, wild creature.

What Noise in the Ancient Silence

I've been hiking this quiet trail for hours
and am surprised as I top a ridge and look
out on a valley with a tall cliff to its north.
The trial I hike descends into the valley.

At the cliff's base is a jumble of gray rocks.
Rocks big as houses, some round with age,
others rough, sharp edged, as if they'd just
fallen from the cliff, maybe this morning.

I imagine that the rocks are a gathering of
wide-tusked mastodons, wooly mammoths,
maybe dire wolves drinking from the creek.
Is it safe to pass these ice-age monsters?

Voices carry softly on the wind to my ear,
breaking the spell of imagination. I search
the valley and notice a pinnacle of rocks
with a small red spot, someone scaling it.

I look back at the boulders under the cliff,
wonder about the monstrous noise those
huge rocks made as they fell, smashing,
bouncing, rolling, in the ancient silence.

With Snow in Tomorrow's Forecast

Buds on the ash, peach, and linden trees
are beginning to swell. Grass that's been
winter-brown the first months of the year
is now showing some hints of green.

The long, evilly-thorned stems of roses
have some green creeping up them,
and the two Japanese maple trees dropped
their leaves, show signs of budding out.

At the end of the alley, where it joins
the sidewalk, honey bees nuzzle the first
of spring's bright, golden dandelions,
a dependable sign that spring has arrived.

Despite the forecast of snow tomorrow.

A Belted Kingfisher

A sudden wild rattle breaks the quiet
as a small blue-gray belted kingfisher,
thinking it's a big bird, issues a warning
to any osprey, eagle, or great blue heron
thinking of fishing in its pond.

It pitches out over the water, hovers,
dives, enters the water head first,
like an Olympic diver, and disappears.
Second later breaking the pond's surface,
it flies straight up, lands on its perch,
and eats a small silver minnow.

The Roan Colt Chases His Shadow

The roan colt frisks across the meadow,
chasing his shadow that the setting sun
is imperceptibly making a bit longer.

He turns at the wooden fence and trots
back to his buckskin dam who stands
in her pool of shadow watching him.

She nuzzles the colt when he gets to her,
and then the two romp playfully around
the meadow, back to where they started.

As day ends, the ridge's shadow slides
past the two grazing horses and takes
their shadows through the meadow,

over the fence, across the road, and up
the ridge to the east. The horses sleep
as evening fades into the starry night.

Dueling Pronghorns on a Fall Morning

The morning sun is warm on my back
and I work up a sweat as I walk this slope.
I've passed through some sage and its
bittersweet aroma mixes with the dust
I've kicked up, scenting the morning air.

Just ahead, off the trail, a pronghorn buck
with his harem of four does stirs nervously.
Just as I think I shouldn't walk any closer,
I notice that the herd isn't watching me
but a buck downslope a quarter mile off.
It's mid fall, rutting season, and I realize
I'm about to see a fight for mating rights.

The harem buck faces the intruder,
lowers his head, paws the ground,
snorts . . .
charges,
hooves
pounding.

He covers the distance in a few seconds.
The challenger barely dodging the charge,
and a second one, then trots off in defeat.

A Red Fox Family Meal

At the tangled snarl of roots
where a wind-downed tree
lies in a sun-bright clearing,
three fox kits play and romp,
growling, wrestling, jumping,
running, suddenly stopping.
Stopping because the vixen
enters in the clearing.

As she approaches, the kits run
to greet her, white-tipped tails
waving their gladness to see her.
She carries a rabbit she's killed,
gives it to them for their lunch.

The largest of the kits, the male,
snarls the other two off and tears
piece after piece from it, eating
wolfishly as his siblings wait.
When he's done, he cleans paws
and muzzle, curls up to sleep
in a small cave in the tree roots.

The female kits now tear pieces
from the rabbit, eating their fill,
then clean themselves and join
their brother in the small cave.

The vixen leaves to hunt again.

Best Not to Get Rattled

A soft slow rattle in the winter-dead grass next to the trail and close to the feet of one of the visitors caught my ear and I gently pulled him away by the arm so as not to startle him and have him jump closer to the snake. The morning was cold enough that the snake's movements were lethargic and even its rattle was weak. It was probably headed for the sunshine on the trail to gather heat to warm its cold blood. We walked away glad that the encounter was safe for all. And the visitors were pleased to see and hear a rattler up close, almost, but not quite, too close.

A Small Black Spider Visits

A black spider, not half the size
of a ladybug, clings to the side
of the sink in my bathroom.

It seems content to sit there,
legs tucked under it, watching
me brush my teeth and shave.

The one thing I do to agitate it
is turn on the water too hard;
perhaps it fears a biblical flood.

I watch it for two mornings,
wondering what it finds to eat
and how long it will remain.

The third morning it's gone,
perhaps down into the dark
of the drain under the plug.

Our Small Hummingbird Feeder

I hung the feeder a week ago, not expecting any hummers for a few more weeks, perhaps halfway through June. Here it's the 3rd of June and the trill of a broad-tailed hummer called my attention to the feeder and there, perched like its owner, was a pretty little broad-tail, dipping his long beak into the sugar water, sipping at times, drinking heartily at others. He came back later, ignored me standing six feet away, for more sipping and drinking. That little bird brought beauty and joy to my day.

The Ancient Peach Blooms Again

Once again this spring its blossoms freeze,
done in by a hard spring cold snap.
Desiccated, they hang on, brown, lifeless,
but this morning tiny green leaves, banners
of hope, appear on the branches, as if the tree
has given the finger to spring for its fickleness.

Originally planted in memory of Mom,
her ashes under its root ball, moved twice,
it survived each time. In early life it fruited
in abundance that broke limbs if we didn't
cull two-thirds of the fruit, juice-dripping-
off-the elbow-and-chin sweet, so plentiful
we gave most away, made peach jelly,
sliced them for cereal, snacks, dessert.

Over the almost 30 years, the peach has lost
two thirds of its limbs, age leaving them dead,
then sawed off. This spring, when the tree filled
again with pink blossoms, it became a bonsai,
an elegant, gray-haired woman, with a beauty
well suited to her age.

As the tree nears the end of its life, it still
blooms each spring, bears fruit in summer.
Age seems now to have sapped its energy.
The fruit doesn't ripen, is not sweet. But it
remains a symbol of hope, of Mom's spirit,
her easy grace, her will to remain loving,
creative, even when enduring great pain,
knowing she was near death.

Mother and Toddler in the Coffee Shop

> *Our eye-beams twisted, and did thread*
> *Our eyes upon one double string*
> From "The Ecstasy" by John Donne

It's eight-fifteen on a sunny spring morning.
Against one wall a line of silent people slouch
intently into the screens of phones and wait
to order their lattes before they go off to work.

Here and there, others stare at screens, text,
read email, ignore the beauty around them.

In the middle of the shop, in a splash of sunlight,
a mother and toddler dance and play and laugh,
glance love-beams at each other. The boy grins,
runs off, spins, laughs back into his mother's arms.

While others continue to stare at their screens.

Hope Is the Thing With feathers

     after Emily Dickinson

Hope is the plea from a young woman,
who has a job interview today, for me
to write a poem about hope, as if that
might create some magic in her life.

Hope is the sparkle in my dog's eyes
as he starts jumping when sees me open
the cellar door where I keep his leash,
thinking I'll take him for a walk.

Hope is the tulip bulbs I plant in fall
while the ground is soft enough to dig
and winter has not yet marched down
from the mountains on frozen feet.

Hope is the grasp of a toddler's hand
on his mother's finger, feeling loved
and protected, as they cross the grass
in the park to the playground.

Hope is the cry on a black mother's lips
as she tells her nineteen-year-old son
to be careful and kisses his cheek as he
heads out the door for the evening.

Hope is the feet of the desperate souls
who endure the scorching Chihuahuan
Desert as they trudge to the wide river
between Ciudad Juarez and El Paso.

*Hope is the feathered thing that perches
in the soul and sings the tune* we want
to hear, the tune that creates magic
for our children and those we love.

An If-only Moment

As he stands next to his wife who chats
with friends about some wonderful sale,
he looks absently at clusters of people
moving thru the hall at the charity event
to a buffet table left or open bar right.

His eyes meet hazel eyes across the hall
belonging to a dark-haired woman who
waits as her husband chats animatedly
with two men whose wives also chat.

Both start as a spark of emotion flares
between them and quickly look away
embarrassed at what they'd felt. They
look back, smile sweetly, nod briefly
at their spouses as if to say, if only.

The Sick Child

>after a painting by Edvard Munch

The young girl tries to comfort her mother,
already grieving her death, reminding her
what she's heard the village priest exclaim
"She's in a better place, in heaven with God."

The mother tries to be brave, not show
the pain she feels, but the last coughing
spell stained the towel red with blood,
and she knows that death is near. She's
collapsed into her pain and her grief.

The painter mirrors the mother's grief
and young girl's fear with dark colors
the mother's dress seems to rise from.
The light between mother and daughter
emphasizes their love and shared pain,
feelings the painter also feels.

The bottle of medicine on the red chest
has not cured the girl, her coughing's
gotten worse. Her pallor's set off by her
blood red hair, suggesting how close
she is to death, the blanket covering her
a mix of muddy colors from the grave.

My Biennial Echocardiogram

I lie on my left side, shirt off, on a high,
narrow, sheeted bed in a small dark room.
Meredith, an echocardiogram tech, holds
a small wand against my ribs that sends
sonar, like a submarine's, into my chest.

Fascinated, I watch a fist-sized muscle,
my heart, pump blood, and listen to its
lub-dub, lub-dub, syncopated rhythm.
I watch sound waves next to thin lines
that show the cycles of my heart's beat.

Meredith captures images of my heart,
records sounds, details my doctor needs.
Her wand looks deeper into my heart
than my doctor's stethoscope, but cannot
see the love or grief or guilt it holds.

A Poem That Doesn't Want To Be Written

I've been looking all morning for a poem
that didn't to want to be written. I read it
a few days ago, but it's disappeared, gone
underground, hiding so I cannot find it.
I looked through all the books I've read
recently but with no luck.

I want to write a poem of spring flowers,
bright yellow tulips, sweet-faced pansies,
a single allium that blooms in the alley,
the sweet scent of lilacs. But I can't start
'til I find that poem to guide me, help me
with mine that doesn't want to be written.

Backyard Sounds

The sounds of traffic on the street
fade as I tune into nature's sounds.
English sparrows chirp incessantly,
competing with the breeze that rattles
the leaves of my neighbor's aspen.
A chattering in the sky announces
a Cooper's hawk hunting nearby
for small birds to feed her young.

A flitter of chickadees whistles pertly
as they search trees for each other.
Two insects fly past quietly, a red admiral
butterfly that tastes my wife's geraniums,
and a dragonfly that looks much like
an ancient biplane fighter on dawn patrol.
The morning sun warms a cicada, who
imitates my neighbor starting her cranky
mower, buzzing once then twice before
belting out a long, droning aria.

The chorus ends abruptly as a fire truck,
siren and klaxon blaring, threads its way
through the intersection, and an airliner
roars overhead from the airport. For a few
relaxing moments, the city sounds hushed,
and those of nature cradled me.

First Love Remembered

He wakes from a short pleasant dream
and smiles at the warmth that spreads
in his slowly dawning consciousness.

In the dream he is once again a young man
in his early 20s, perhaps in college, perhaps
just out, and he meets a young woman who

seems as attracted to him as he is to her.
They chat a bit and he wakes. He drifts off
again and she is still there, smiling at him.

He drifts in and out of the dream and she
is there each time, until he finally wakes
and lies there thinking about his first love.

She was also attracted to him. They first met
and danced at noon in the high school gym,
both shy, and he's not sure if he asked her

or if she asked him to dance. He remembers
her shy smile, her warmth against his body
as they danced, the tingle as their hands met.

They dated that spring into summer when he
moved away and he never saw her again.
But he remembers the sweet feeling of first love.

Lament of the Jilted #2 Dixon Ticonderoga

How did I wind up with my life like this, ignored
and collecting dust in an unused black coffee mug
printed with "Life isn't about finding yourself,
it's about creating yourself"? It started out so well.

When we were in first grade and Mrs. Kenneth
was teaching us to write the alphabet, he held me
tightly in his chubby fingers, so tightly at times
that I could hardly breathe. They were good days.

Every morning, he'd reach in his desk, take me out,
sharpen my point, wipe the dirt from my eraser,
write letters, then words in his *Big Chief* tablet,
tongue hanging out in his sweet childhood effort.

We were a team then. And later in fourth grade,
Miss Palmer was teaching us how to write cursive.
We spent our mornings together. He held me tightly
again, tongue out, as he formed many new words.

And then through high school and college I was his
constant companion. He took me from room to room,
lecture to lecture, taking notes, writing in blue books,
and also filling in little black circles as he took tests.

His philandering began in college, as he picked up
with a mechanical pencil, spending nights with her.
Then he dumped her for a Bic ball point pen, later
a roller ball, and finally a phone and computer.

So, for the past thirty years, I've stood in this cup,
gathering dust with a dried-up Bic ball point pen,
Pentel roller ball, and Sharpie highlighter. Maybe
he holds me twice a year. Oh! Oh! The heartbreak!

An Old Typewriter's Memories

I've been sitting here in my case,
unused, for God knows how long.
I wound up here in the garage attic
when the family moved to the city.

My typist and I had spent many
nights together though four years
of college and two stints in grad
school as we typed those papers
for classes, always hurried, often
the night before they were due.

We typed letters to family, friends,
school papers for his two children,
letters of recommendation, and job
applications in those busy years.

He'd take me from my case, set me
gently on his desk, roll some paper
onto my platen, lay fingers gently
on my keys, and then start typing,
often dozens of pages as he deftly
stroked my keys, watching letters,
words, sentences, paragraphs, form
on the paper. I often giggled to hear
him swear when he typed too fast
and jammed my keys.

But after working together for years,
an awful thing happened to ruin it;
he learned computers were easier
to use. He shut my case years ago
and hasn't let me out since.

The Moon by Earthlight

As I'm on my way to pick up
tacos, a low crescent moon
winks at me in the darkening
sky through the tree branches,
a message in code semaphored
from ship to ship in wartime.

When I get to Taco Bell, I gawk
at the moon's silver crescent
and faint outline in the night
sky lit by earthshine, sunlight
reflected off earth to the moon.

If people lived on the moon,
could a couple fall in love
while strolling hand in hand
in the dark by earthlight?

A Brief Scent of Rain

The sky closed down, dark and thick.
Wind hissed in the trees and they danced.
The finches at the feeders flew to a nearby
ash, except for one who perched briefly
on a wire and sang. A squirrel on the wall
ducked out of sight.

The day cooled and filled with the scent
of rain. The hiss of the wind in the trees
became the hiss of a hard rain on leaves
and grass. A faint mist tickled my arms.

The afternoon seemed somehow to change,
trees moved closer, backyard grew smaller.
The sound of the rain drowned the racket
of traffic and the city. Twenty minutes later
the rain slacked, city noises intruded again,
and the finches returned to the feeders.

But that brief scent of rain took me to a small
meadow thirty years ago, a hastily set up tent
that my son and I crawled into as a hard rain
started pelting it as thunder had been pelting
our ears for an hour. We lay on sleeping bags,
and fell asleep to that sound on the tent fly
and the hiss of rain on mountain ponderosa.

The Winter Solstice

Today the sun halts its journey south
to start back north. But it's earth's axis
that is tipped north, making it seem
the sun's been going south.

The earth appears fixed in space to us,
so we think that the sun rises in the east,
sets in the west, stops its descent south,
and its climb north at the two solstices.
But it's the rotation and wobble of this
old planet that makes all this happen.

As the earth spins around its axis,
the sun only seems to rise and set.
The earth's axis wobbles each year,
moving south in spring and summer
making days longer, moving north
in fall and winter. Days seem shorter.

Our inflated sense of our importance
makes us think that the solar system
and starry universe revolve around
this tiny blue dot that's lost in space.

A Spring Afternoon in January

One day left in January but this week's
weather has seemed more like there's
only one more day left to go in March.

A bit over a week ago a foot of snow
covered the lawns, streets were packed
snow and ice. We were deep into winter.

Now, we've had a bit more than a week
of days with highs in the 50s, cool nights
in the mid 30s, days of blue sky and sun.

The snow has melted quickly, patches
of grass have been tricked into greening,
street intersections now are small lakes.

On our walks, we're tempted to look for
the first purple crocuses, daffodils, trees
leafing out, birds back from the south.

But winter is back with cold and snow
on Tuesday night, continuing through
Wednesday. Winter's April-fools joke.

The Backyard on a Cold January Day

The lawn hides under patches of icy snow
left behind by two storms a few weeks ago.
The morning sun's so weak these days, just
a bright circle in the winter-gray overcast.

Frozen leaves hang from the maple trees,
looking almost as pitiful as the dead ones
on the clematis vines clinging to the garage.
The ash and peach trees have a leaf or two
hanging on them, ones that even the stiff
winter winds have failed to pry loose.

The bird feeders, newly filled, attracted
chickadees who call to others to announce
food is handy, sunflower and mixed seeds.
Some seeds drop to the ground as birds eat,
and squirrels are the clean-up crew, eating
the seeds as fast as birds spill them.

The drum feeder's nearly been destroyed
by hungry flickers and I'll replace it.

A Sunday Afternoon in Early March

When you brought in the UPS delivery, you left
the front door ajar and a ray of sunlight snuck in
to lay on the rug by the door. I'd been cooped up
all week, and that gold spot of sun invited me
to go outside to a Sunday in early March.

Pampas grass that all summer stood green and
head high is now sere, weighted by two snows
into a tumble of stalks, tilted toward a small pile
of icy snow, shoveled there by the man who
cleared the walk.

The weeping mulberry, leafless, forlorn, looks
defeated, its canes bent toward the ground and
echoing the brown of the winter-dead grasses.
The blue spruce leans against the house
in its winter torpor.

The hardy yellow and purple pansies planted
in the fall have not yet recovered from a long
burial beneath the slowly melting snow.

But some signs that spring will soon be here
are the maniacal laugh of a flicker sitting atop
an elm, calling for a mate, and three doors off,
children's bubbly laughter.

Warming in the Early Spring Sun

I sit on the second step of the back porch,
leaning against the top step, thinking,
while watching the pup chase a squirrel.

She comes back and sits next to me,
watching the squirrel she just chased
sneak back down the tree to the feeder.

Then she leans into me, a bonding move,
I think, so I put an arm over her, give her
a hug, and scratch her under the chin.

We both enjoy the sun's rays warming us,
absorbing their energy. The pup quickly
uses it up chasing that squirrel again.

Spring Dawn at Monte Vista

The sky brightens in the east and water
in flooded fields reflects morning light,
showing the hundreds of sandhill cranes
who start calling to each other.

Off in the distance a few cranes begin to fly,
spiraling into early spring. More birds rise
and call to others to join the journey north
to distant fields where they'll nest and mate.

The vortex expands. Soon the fields, pink
with the reflection of the gathering sunrise,
are almost empty. The noise of the cranes
increases, almost too loud for human ears.

Then, as the birds head north by northwest
in thin wavering lines, a meadowlark sings.

A Bluebird Morning on the Prairie

The spring morning is sun-bright, calm, with a slight breeze, not even strong enough to cause the husks on last year's milkweed to rattle. A meadowlark sings from a mullein stalk thirty yards to the left of the trail and a red-tailed hawk's slurring cry calls our attention to where it circles near a lone cottonwood where its mate broods eggs. I walk with two visitors and point out a small herd of pronghorn that disappears quickly into a drainage between two ridges. As we walk through the western wheatgrass and little bluestem to see spring's white six-petaled sand lilies, the sweet scent of sage follows us.

A Summer Morning's Gift

From the shade of a tree, I look
into the green, sun-filled yard.

I'm stunned by four translucent wings
and a body lightly brushed with gold.

A passing dragonfly quietly hovers,
A gift from God, haloed by the sun.

Swallowtail

Hey you,
tiger swallowtail over there,
fluttering your bright yellow wings,
lifting slowly into the shade
of that ash tree.

Are you, like me,
just looking for a cool, quiet place
to hang out
this hot July afternoon?

Or do you sense the closing of your short life,
the few hours you have left to fly,
the need to lay your eggs on some leaves
in the dark of that ash?

I hope you'll leave young for us to watch
their daily fluttering visits,
their delicate buoyant beauty,
at the end of our summer,
into fall.

A Good Summer in the Rear View Mirror

The peach begins to drop gold leaves on the grass
and the purple petunias have folded their tents,
but brown-eyed susans in the same pot have not.
Next to the fountain, the pink impatiens have not
lost their luster, and the geraniums are still gaudy.

Feeders have been busy with chickadees visiting
every day, sharing seeds with tiny nuthatches
and downy woodpeckers. Bluejays visit often,
their jay, jay, jay echoing through the yard.
The jays respect the long bills of the flickers
and wait their turn to eat.

Finches sit for long stretches in the feeder,
cracking open and eating sunflower seeds.
A Cooper's hawk comes one afternoon,
snatches up a finch landing on a feeder,
flies off with it in its talons.

Squirrels are busy in the grass eating seeds
birds scattered. Our pup has tried all summer
for a squirrel meal but has never caught one.

Days start darker and cooler since the sun's past
the equinox. Air feels and smells of fall, as earth
starts its autumnal slide into winter.

As Summer Ends

wandering hawk
ascends some spiral stairs
a spirit bird

days are quieter
cicadas are not droning
did they all find mates

sunflowers
in morning shade
look confused

the bees have gone
after this strange summer
their harvest is in

stiff north breeze
with a bit of a bite
a taste of fall

summer's bright petals
fade and fold into themselves
a grandmother's hands

first fall moon
low in the predawn west
waves to summer leaving

The Wildlife Refuge Eases into Fall

Autumn nights have yet to suffer a hard frost
so the older trees, elms, oaks, and cottonwoods
have not yet started to turn. But younger ones
planted in the open area along a small creek
on the refuge's south border are bright yellow.

The long treeless stretches of lion-tawny grass
are marked with patches of ochre where plants
have lost their green. The breeze whispers softly
in tall stalks of western wheat grass and flutters
the pale leaves of little blue stem grass.

A dozen bison graze on buffalo grass and blue grama.
The new calves have lost their copper-penny color
and are now dusky brown, half the size of their dams.
A colony of prairie dogs barks and stands at attention,
watching me as I slowly drive by.

Silence presages the death of the grasses in winter
while the nearby stream flows softly like the wind.
The deep blue sky belies the chilly bite to the wind,
and off in the distant hazy west, the mountain peaks
have already donned their ermine stoles.

A Walk on an Indian Summer Day

I find myself grouchy, moody, not creative
and know that time in nature often cures.
But I'm city bound and it's too late to drive
east on the prairie or west to the mountains.

So I lace up my shoes, grab my keys, don
a hoodie, and head out the back gate into
a beautiful, sunny, autumn afternoon that
feels a lot like Indian summer.

A rose in my yard has put forth two last
blooms, both blown, pansies are mostly
covered in bright gold maple leaves, but
yellow and purple faces smile through,

and the sun shines in an iris blue sky.
As I warm up and take off my hoodie,
the sun is comforting on my bare arms,
and a light breeze is at my back for now.

To the north, a buttermilk sky drifts off
to the northeast, and what earlier were
mountain wave clouds to the west have
become soft altocumulus cotton candy.

I slosh through deep puddles of yellow
and red ash, elm, oak, and maple leaves.
They scatter in waves from my shoes
as if I were splashing through water.

Many neighbors also walk this fine
Saturday afternoon, nodding politely,
not wanting to spoil the peaceful mood
or miss hearing the music in the trees.

When I reach home, my mood's changed.
I smile at the pansies and thank the rose
for its blossoms this summer. The walk
proved to be the balm I hoped it would.

A Trip to the Prairie to Enjoy Its Fall Colors

Thirty miles east of the city, on roads that change
from asphalt to dirt to teeth-jarring washboard,
we turn south on county road 161. A mile past a gate,
we rattle over a cattle guard and stop.
A hundred feet below and a half mile southeast,
gold-leafed cottonwoods line wandering West Bijou Creek.

As we drive carefully down the steep, winding hill
to the valley floor, we're surrounded by fall wildflowers.
There's the yellow of sunflowers and blanketflowers.
The purples and blues of gayfeather, knapweed,
verbena, asters, lupine, and groundcherry.
In a drainage with Canada and bull thistles,
monarch butterflies flutter around pink milkweed.

Below, in an arroyo, a mule deer buck and three does
race away. Above, riding wind that climbs the ridge,
a golden eagle hunts for cottontails and jackrabbits.
On the valley floor a pronghorn buck watches
over his harem of six does. A younger buck,
hoping to steal a doe or two, hangs out nearby,
eyed by the nervous harem buck.

We drive slowly past a large prairie dog colony.
The prairie dogs bark at us, at a red-tailed hawk
who circles overhead, at a ferruginous hawk
perched on a fence post. A coyote stalks near
a cluster of burrows; a badger patrols the other side.
Prairie dogs stand at attention, watch, bark.

The harvest full moon will soon rise, so we drive back
to a tiny picnic area, grill burgers, chat, wait for moonrise.
At sunset, lenticular clouds flare into burnt orange
and crimson, fade to pink then gray.

A meadowlark closes the day with a quiet evensong.
As the moon clears the horizon, a nearby coyote howls.
Two others answer. By the creek, in the cottonwoods,
a great-horned owl hoots. Here, a lonely cricket chirps.

Collapsed Barn

The barn, brought low by time and snow, has settled sadly like a sailing ship, long stranded on a bar. It once sheltered cows and horses and sheep from blizzards and drought. Now it's a pile of boards in the grass that reclaims the land. The family who lived here left small evidence of their passing. A barely visible trail in the grass leads to trees by the creek. Three children and a wife are buried there, headstones flattened by the '65 floods. A low concrete rectangle tells where they once dreamed, loved, and hoped. Two pregnant mule deer watch me from the trees. They and the sand lilies at my feet—faint signs of hope.

As I Walk Through Aztec Ruins

It's a planned and engineered structure of four
hundred rooms, most for living, some for storage,
a great kiva for tribal ceremonies, smaller ones
for clans, built skillfully in rows of stones hauled
more than five miles to the site, earth colored,
and appearing to grow out of the ground.

They cut large timbers for vigas in the great kiva,
hauled them twenty miles from ponderosa forests.
Hauled smaller ones from aspen and piñon stands
to build door and window frames, form roofs.
They hauled water from the nearby Animas river
to mix with sand and crushed rock for mortar.
They laid the north wall of the west complex
so it aligns perfectly with the summer solstice,
then inlaid green stones in the walls for beauty.

The ancient Puebloans who built these structures
left home in Chaco Canyon, seventy miles south,
for reasons we can only guess at. A long drought,
Apache attacks, the next move on their spiritual
migration? They spent three decades building
this structure, lived in it for two centuries, farming
the semi-arid land around it, then moved on.

Their descendants now live in dozens of pueblos
along the Rio Grande to the east, the Acoma, Hopi,
and Zuni pueblos to the south. The Pueblo people
do not consider these structures abandoned ruins,
but as a resting place on their ancestors' migration.
They revere it because ancestral Puebloan spirits
still abide here.

I'm awestruck with reverence as I look and listen.

The Ancient Call of Sandhill Cranes

As we hike up the steep, narrow ravine
I point to mule deer tracks in the mud,
mud left by an infrequent autumn rain
in the shadow of the Rocky Mountains.

I show the hikers the prairie gay feather,
its dainty foot-long pink stalks, fall asters
hugging the sand, tall sunflowers waving
in a slight breeze, native wavy-leaf thistle.

The only sound is the crunch of our boots
on the sandy trail, the swish of blue grama
and western wheatgrass against our boots,
the call of a red-tailed hawk high above us.

The quiet of the fall afternoon, its low sun
at our backs, is broken by very faint calls,
familiar, ancient, insistent, growing louder.
Then over the ridge comes a line of cranes.

The sandhills call to each other as if they
fear we might offer some danger to them.
Something in their calls sounds urgent yet
calming to me, calling me to somewhere.

I step off the trail, mouth agape, watching
the ragged line of cranes, calling, calling.
Prehistoric looking birds, all neck and legs,
their wings stroking the air ever so smoothly.

I'm transported to a calm place in memory,
a narrow, sheer waterfall where a mountain
stream drops a thousand feet onto the rocks,
and then disappears under jungle foliage.

As the calls of the cranes fade, I fly again
over that waterfall near the *Song Re* valley,
a place that seems far from the war, where
nature's peace restored my shattered soul.

A Day Along the Rio Grande

As the sun sets and darkness rises
from the rocky floor of the canyon,
we scour the hillside for firewood
amid the scent of piñon and juniper.

It's been a glorious autumn day
in this canyon sculpted from granite
by the headwaters of a rushing river.
We are enthralled by nature's beauty.

The coming night will not be silent
as the burble and splash of water
on rocks in the mountain stream
will continue throughout the dark.

We gather round a rock-ringed fire
for the warmth of burning wood,
aroma of simmering beef stew, and
sizzle of grilling rainbow trout.

After we eat, we heat water to wash
dishes, sharing stories and jokes,
then crawl into sleeping bags, lulled
to sleep by the murmuring river.

Growing up on Long Island

I grew up on an island surrounded
by water, the Long Island Sound
to the north, Atlantic Ocean east
and south, East River to the west.

Fishing is a major industry there,
and many men fished on days off,
weekends, and summer vacations.
They fished for flounder, bluefish,
striped bass, cod, tuna, mahi-mahi.

My retired Uncle Bill went fishing
three or four days a week, offering
us anything he caught because he
and Aunt Ella couldn't eat it all.

I was raised Catholic, so on Fridays
we couldn't eat meat. My mother
fixed a fish dish that day, usually
elbow macaroni, mayonnaise,
chopped onions, carrots, celery,
and salmon or tuna from a can.

My Disastrous First Day in First Grade

Our three-room country school didn't have
kindergarten, so my first day was first grade.
Mom drove me to school that day--the only
time I think--and walked me into the first
and second grade room to meet Mrs. Kenneth.
Mom told her if I misbehaved to spank me,
send home a note. She'd spank me again.

At lunchtime, not knowing school rules,
I climbed over a five-foot chain link fence
from the noisy, schoolyard playground
to the quiet front yard. I got spanked,
brought home a note, got spanked again.

I thought both these spankings unfair
because I didn't know the school rules
and also didn't know that the vine that
climbed that fence too was poison ivy.

Grade School in a Small Village

He didn't like school but enjoyed the mile and a half walk to and from by himself. He watched cows and horses in the fields and waved to farmers and their sons driving Farmall or Fordson tractors. In the winter he had fun running a few steps in his galoshes and then sliding on snow-covered roads, the snow packed hard by cars, or just shuffling through fluffy new snow before cars packed it down.

The time he spent sitting at his desk in a row of brown wooden desks with wrought iron legs that had his books, pencils, and red *Big Chief Tablet* in it dragged, emphasized by the slow tick . . . tick . . . tick . . . of the big *Standard* clock on the wall by the windows. He looked forward to the walk back home and playing in the trees behind his house.

The Steaming Manure Pile

Mornings growing up, I walked to school
and passing Joe Manetta's farm smelled
the manure pile. It grew and grew all year,
summer, fall, and winter when it steamed
as warm manure was added from the cows.

Near the pile stood an unpainted wagon
with wooden, iron-rimmed wheels. It sat,
never seeming to move. In late winter or
early spring it moves a bit each day
and the manure pile got smaller.

That old wagon was a manure spreader,
and it fertilized Manetta's fields that then
were planted with vegetable crops sold
at their tiny wooden roadside stand and
at city markets and local grocery stores.

This was in the tradition of family farms.
Cows for milk and their manure spread
in the fields by horses pulling spreaders.
Manetta's one concession to technology,
a red Farmall tractor replaced the horse.

The Slow Crawl of Time

He squirms on the hard wooden seat
and watches the other kids in his row
of third graders work on the exercise.

He's finished it quickly and is bored,
hears Miss Palmer give the next row,
one of fourth graders, an assignment.

When she finishes with the fourth grade,
she bends to her own work at her desk,
probably grading what the fifth graders

had finished earlier. His day drags on
measured by the tick . . . tick . . . tick . . .
of the clock on the wall over his head.

He's dreaming of playing after school,
and is startled when Miss Palmer raises
her voice, calling him for a third time.

She asks him to recite the five-times
table, which he does, having learned
the times tables with his mother's help.

Her exercise for the third grade ends,
and he works on the new assignment.
She then works with the fifth graders.

He quickly finishes, squirming again,
as the clock's tick . . . tick . . . tick . . .
measures out the slow crawl of time.

My Childhood Memories Are Rare

and those that include my parents even
rarer. Perhaps because I was a loner,
playing by myself, and they were not
the type to get on the floor and play.
They were more the type who believed

Spare the rod,
        and spoil the child.
                Children should be seen
                      and not heard.

I do have one set of intense memories
that include my mother and start with her
pulling me across her lap, taking down
my pants, and whaling on my bare bottom
with the back of her Bakelite hairbrush,

        whack
                after whack
                        after painful whack

The memories include the blinding pain,
my hot tears, my screams for her to stop,
and my feeling of not being much loved.

But I forget what it was that I did wrong.

A Little Night Music

Childhood summers were magical for me
as I got to play outside all day, climb trees,
ride my bike, explore the woods behind our
house. As it got dark my mother would call
me into the house to clean up and go to bed.

And the magic continued there in my attic
bedroom, where through the open window
I'd hear crickets chirp their songs of longing.
And most nights I'd hear the iconic music
of my childhood, the whip-poor-will, who
would sing his evening Gregorian chant.

Often as I'd almost drift off, I'd hear the wail
of a steam locomotive at a grade crossing or
signaling its arrival at the Stony Brook station
to the north or Ronkonkoma to the south.
Then the chug-a, chug-a, chug, chug, chug
as the train steamed out of the station.

Once in a while we'd have a thunderstorm.
First I'd hear its grumble, waking me, then
I'd begin to see lightning flashes. When rain
started, I'd hear the first few, raindrops plop
on the roof a few feet above my head followed
by the steady downpour as the storm arrived.
Those sounds still put me to sleep, smiling.

Winter nights were longer, not only because
the sun came up later and set earlier, but also
because I had school and went to bed earlier.
Night music was mostly absent then because
my bedroom window was closed.

But one winter sound still echoes in my head,
the sound of a county snow plow's roar as it

passes down our road, blade scraping along
the rough surface of the oiled country road.

And although I have very few sights or smells
that bring back good memories of childhood,
the whistle of a train, thunder in the night, or
the roar of a snowplow along the parkway,
bring back that country night music.

They Called Me the Big Rock

I lie here about a hundred-fifty feet
from a divided, four-lane highway,
near a small pedestal with a plate
on it that describes how I got here.

The description says the retreating
glacier at the end of the Wisconsin
ice age, twenty thousand years ago,
left me here, a large, gray erratic.

It does not say seventy-five years
ago, I was in the middle of an oak
forest with no roads or buildings
near me, only a thin winding path.

It does not say a gray-haired woman
sat here, surrounded by four or five
kids, eight or ten years old, eating
peanut butter and jelly sandwiches.

It does not say she led them here
every summer, new ones joining
the group as older ones outgrew
the adventure and the long hike.

And it does not say his memories
of sitting here with his grandma,
eating sandwiches, would rescue
his mind from the insanity of war.

Karl's Old McCormick Deering Tractor

had steel wheels that were six feet high
with six-inch spikes welded onto them
to give more traction in muddy terrain.

The tractor was about 30 years old
and its bright red paint was a mixture
of peeling red flakes and a lot of rust.

Karl got it at an auction from a farm
that failed because of the depression
when the banks called in their loans.

He also got a horse-drawn sickle-bar
mower and rake, and shortened their
tongues so the tractor could pull them.

One late summer afternoon after lunch,
Karl cranked that old brute of a tractor
to life and it belched smoke as it started.

He climbed up in the tractor's seat and
I got on the mower and we drove down
a dirt road to a twenty-acre alfalfa field.

At the end of each swath we cut, I'd step
on a pedal that engaged a cog that used
the wheel's motion to lift the mower arm.

I'd catch a lever and hold that heavy arm
up as Karl drove to the far side of the field
and we'd cut alfalfa in the other direction.

A few days later we returned to the field,
this time with the hay rake, raking across
the alfalfa, putting it in parallel windrows.

When the alfalfa was dry, the tractor pulled
an old wagon that we'd pitch the hay onto,
to bring in winter feed for Karl's cows.

A Small Green Studebaker

Today, as I'm stopped for a red light,
a big blue Ford 150 sits in front of me,
a large Silverado idles on my left side,
a hulking black RAM too close behind,
all too shiny to have ever worked a day.

My last summer in high school I'd be
at the dairy at dawn, get into a small
green Studebaker loaded with crates,
twelve bottles of unpasteurized milk
each. We'd head out to deliver them.

At each stop, Karl would tell me how
many bottles of milk, or buttermilk,
to deliver. I'd lean into the pickup bed,
load them into a wire carrier, run them
to milk boxes, bring back the empties.

Karl and his wife, Carola, are long dead.
The pasture of black and white Holsteins
and barn replaced by rows of look-alike
houses, filling stations, and strip-malls.

But I smile to remember the sweet smell
of the dairy at dawn, the heft and clink
of milk bottles as I'd run them to a house,
then back to that small green Studebaker.

First Flight

First flight:
the escape of
Icarus from the maze
with his wings of feathers and wax.
Too high!

Kill Devil Hill, December 17, 1903

Tiny sparks generated by magnetos ignite
the fuel-air mixture that's been compressed
by pistons in cylinders of two small engines.

Heat from the burning fuel expands the air
in the cylinders, forcing the pistons down,
pushing on two crankshafts, rotating them.

Propellers at the end of those crankshafts
bite into the air, propel the fragile biplane.
Orville flies 120 feet in 12 seconds.

Learning to Spin the T-37

We'd heard before we started flying
the T-37 jet trainer, that it could get
into a spin difficult to recover from,
so difficult that it could easily crash.

On my first flight, to dispel my fears,
my instructor put our T-37 into a spin,
pushing the stick far forward to make it
spin faster
and faster,
around
and around
and around
so fast
it
was
hard
to
tell
which
way
we
spun.

He took his hands off the controls
and it meekly stopped spinning.

He had me spin the T-37 and recover
several times, to give me confidence
that I could recover from any spin.

He even suggested that I practice
spins when solo so I'd remember
how to get out of an accidental one.

North of Greenville, MS, July, 1960

I'd been practicing *a hundred things you
have never dreamed of,* and I decided I'd
sightsee from three thousand feet up.
A gray smudge of smoke caught my eye,
drew me north, to find a house burning.
I had no way to call the fire department
and could only hope that someone had,
that help was on its way.

A bit further north I saw off to the west
the Arkansas river, making its slow way
to the Mississippi and on to New Orleans,
its brown waters, muddy with snowmelt
from the prairie, to join the clear waters
of the Mississippi, its spring freshet gone,
and the two rivers flowed hand-in-hand
for miles, each on its own side of the bed.

Then I saw a strange sight a bit southeast,
a field that looked like it had snow on it,
so I headed there but soon realized it was
a cotton field, with its white cotton bolls.
I could see where a line of people picking
the cotton had stripped the snow from
part of the field, in the southeast corner,
where a gray, unpainted shack leaned
into the mid-morning sun and a wisp
of smoke told that the sharecropper's
woman was getting kids off to school.

Then the clock on the panel said time
for me to head to the base and land.
But I still carry those images with me.

> With a line borrowed from *High Flight.*

One Dark October Night, 1962

At 26 thousand feet over the Atlantic, we
follow the lead tanker five hundred feet
below, a mile in front of us. We're on our
second of this night's three-hour missions.
And we flew two of them last night.

In the inky dark, other than a few stars,
the only lights we see are the red rotating
beacons and red and green running lights
of lead and a bomber, so small against
the cold black void of the north Atlantic.

Far to the south, in waters near Cuba,
the Navy has set a blockade to stop
Russian cargo ships carrying missiles
to Cuba. We came off a week of alert
just two days ago, primed to launch
if the Russian ships refuse to stop.

A bomber slides into position behind
and below us. Our boom operator flies
the fuel nozzle down into the refueling
receptacle. I open six valves, switch on
four pumps, pass one hundred twenty
thousand pounds of fuel to the bomber.

It's barely three in the morning when
we finish. The bombers fly east and we
fly west to our base and land exhausted.
Tomorrow we'll go back on alert.

Flying As a Gift, a New Way of Seeing

When she was learning to fly, her attention was
focused on the horizon, the airplane's attitude,
on using the controls, where the airfield was.
But, after a few solo landings, her instructor
said to go up and just enjoy flying.

She looks, sees the layout of the town, how it's
shaped by ridges, the river, that Main Street is
longer than D Avenue and leads out of town
on the state highway. How D ends by a ridge
at one end, the river at the other.

The wood behind her house is much smaller
than remembered from childhood wanderings.
Her house and grade school also seem smaller.

And the high school looks smaller, its buildings,
the oval cinder track, the field where she watched
football on Fridays, played lacrosse in the fall,
and the student parking lot that seemed to go on
forever if she was late and parked at the far end.

The radio crackles, startling her as another pilot
calls that he's entering the traffic pattern to land,
pulling her attention away from the vista below
to the clock, and she sees it's time for her to land.

She turns to head for the dairy, the checkpoint
she uses to line up for the traffic pattern, calls
the tower, and descends to the proper altitude,
notes that the view she's been exploring shrinks
as she descends to land.

Flying Gliders from a Grass Field

When spring finally came to Virginia, it seemed to come all at once, flowers bursting out in loud hallelujahs. Winter rains stopped and the pasture we flew out of in late spring, summer, and fall dried out and greened up so we moved the planes and gliders from the paved runway at Culpepper to a lovely grass field in Winchester. Oh the joy of gentle touchdowns in grass rather than the noisy, jarring ones on pavement.

There were two hazards, though, in the grass. The first was stepping on a still-soft cow pie left from early spring when cows grazed there. The second was wood ticks that crawled out of the grass and up pant legs. I flew in shorts so I could feel them crawling up my legs and pitch them out the window before they burrowed into me. I knew they couldn't fly, so I wondered if they fell softly enough to enjoy the several thousand foot fall into the grass.

Consider the Wind

It is a quiet Sunday morning and I sit outside
on the patio writing and thinking about wind.
It is one of the first days this summer I'm able
to write outside because the smoke and ozone
have made the air unhealthy. The wind must
have shifted, carrying the smoke away, and
the air is predicted to contain less ozone.

As a pilot I've spent hours buffeted by the wind,
hindered or aided by it, yet have never seen it.
I've watched the Japanese maple dance with it,
felt it in my hair, heard it rustle in the ash trees
in the backyard, sing in wind chimes, smelled it
when it blows from the Purina cat food plant,
seemed even to taste it when I'm grilling steaks.

It could be visitors from the spirit world,
like angels, dancing on the head of a pin.

Birth of a Thunderstorm

All morning a line of small cumulus clouds
forms over the range of hills west of town,
the sun painting them a brilliant white.

By mid-afternoon some clouds have grown
large, towering over the peaks so quickly
we watch them in awe as they balloon.

One cloud sails off from the brown ridge,
catches the west wind and eases onto
the plains, a presence to be noted,
a storm that walked on legs of lightning,
dragging its shaggy belly over the fields.

The first few drops smack like gunshots,
then the bedlam quickly becomes deafening.
The storm finally moves east, taking its fury,
leaving only the kiss of a lingering shower.

      Italic lines borrowed from Ted Kooser's poem "Mother."

I Ride the Wind

My student was holding a steady
position in our glider behind the
tow plane when it quickly jumped
as it hit some fast rising air. I took
control, put us back into position,
and noted where the lift was so I
could use it later to climb higher.

The rising air was like a fast stream,
with water flowing over a large rock,
to create a wave that doesn't move.
We got off tow at a thousand feet,
turned into the wave, and tacked
back and forth across it. It lifted
us up over ten thousand feet with
no engine, impressing my student.

Years later, I climbed into a sailplane
at the foot of the Rockies wearing
winter clothes and an oxygen mask.
I got off tow at nine thousand feet,
three thousand above the runway.
The tow plane did that same jump
I'd seen years earlier so I knew that
I'd found a wave to climb in.

That wave took me to more than
twenty-three thousand feet. Even
with heavy mittens and battery-
heated socks, my hands and feet
were freezing in the cold air. But,
at more than nine thousand feet
above Pikes Peak I was smiling.

How I Miss My Flying Days

Sometimes on my daily walk when I hear
an airliner roar overhead, climbing from
the Denver airport or watch a sun-dazzled
contrail silently inch its way across the sky,
I miss those, long-ago, sunlit days when I
could have been piloting one of those birds.

I miss watching the earth slowly unroll
under me, towns, cities, lakes, rivers,
mountains, roads, train tracks heading
to places I'd likely never visit, imagining
what life might be like in the small village
that's just passing under my left wing.

At night, over the great plains or llano,
I'd wonder about the family that lives by
that light miles away from other lights.
Maybe a solitary soul trying to escape
the crush and stink of the city, a retired
couple missing kids and grandkids.

Flying over Canada, I saw vast roadless
forests north of the St. Lawrence River,
with narrow cuts in them for railroads
to distant towns. I'd see huge expanses
of snow fields in the winter and wonder
why anyone would choose to live there.

On several trips across the Pacific, I saw
ships crossing it, knowing they took days
to traverse what I would fly over in hours.
But I knew the anxiety of flying for hundreds
of miles with no checkpoints to know I was
on track to an infinitesimally small island.

Just as I explored on my bike as a teenager,

I explored on wings during my flying days.
I miss those many hours when I flew over
places I had read about, wondered about,
adding to the map I carried in my head,
read now only from an airliner's window.

Memoir

I pull a book down from the shelf,
a memoir I wrote twenty years ago
about my war thirty years earlier,
more than half my lifetime ago.

As I read, I'm reminded of places,
people, battles, emotions, I knew
and felt, the elation, anger, humor,
sorrow, and fear from that war.

I review those emotions, both
good and bad, and realize that
those madcap events helped
shape the person I am today

A Quiet Morning Over Vietnam

I add power, lift the tailwheel, and at 55
ease back on the stick, and my little bird
jumps off the runway. The sun's not up,
but the eastern sky's becoming lighter.
As I turn south, I see the purple bulge
of hills and mountains off to my right.

I continue to climb, then turn to the west.
The sun now gilds distant mountain tops,
but has not yet reached the lower hills.
It paints the circle of my propeller gold
as I climb into its light. The land below
is a quilt of light and dark rice paddies.

The radio's quiet and the tower's not yet
open for work. No other airplanes seem
to be in the air. Or maybe like me, others
enjoy the silence and morning light before
the day's battles and emergencies begin.

I level at fifteen hundred feet, ease off
power, set the trim to keep the plane
steady, turn southwest, begin my day.

English 405, Grad School, May 1970

We were all trying to hide, those of us
who had served in that unpopular war.
Many of us had been ostracized a time
or two, so we strove to fit in, unnoticed.

There was another reason to stay hidden;
the National Guard had killed four students
demonstrating against the war I'd just come
back from a few days before at Kent State.

It was a teach-in day, one to discuss the war,
the Kent State shootings, the nation's anger,
and why the New Mexico National Guard
was on our campus, bayonets on their rifles.

I sat, hiding in sight, listening to the angry
rhetoric and questions others had until Jim,
our prof, who knew I had been to Vietnam,
asked me to share my experiences with them.

Anger at Jim evaporated as I told of my role,
anger at being ostracized when I returned,
and I saw students' attitudes toward me change
as they accepted me as a scarred human being.

After the Interview

The teenage neighbor who shovels the snow
from our walks asks if he can interview me
about my experiences in Vietnam for a school
report. We meet at Starbucks to chat.

We discuss several types of missions I flew there,
how most were quiet with no action, while some
were filled with flames, explosions, death, fear,
and joy over lives I helped to save — raw emotions.

I tell him that combat was an adrenaline rush that
lasted for several hours or days, followed by grief
over friends killed, guilt over men I helped kill,
and guilt for the pain of wives, children, families.

What I don't expect is that the interview causes
a bit of rush of adrenaline, like that of battles.
I get home feeling good that I helped him learn
about my war so he can write his report.

But I don't expect that I'll once more feel the grief
and guilt of that war so deeply. Like cockleburs
in the wild stuck to socks, emotional seeds cling
to talk of missions I'd flown, battles I'd fought.

They come back that night, hang around for days,
until, like cockleburs, I pick them off, one by one,
pricking my soul as I do, often drawing blood.

Mom's Old Peach Tree

Mom's old peach tree
half dead
but . . . ah . . . blossoms

peach tree blooms
have weathered snow and cold
their pink joy

low morning sunlight
sets the peach blossoms aglow
like alabaster

the peach tree
adds a lime green scarf
to pink blossoms

the peach tree hums
with wings of bees
spring's song

the bonsai shape
of the ancient peach tree
its petals falling

My Mother-in-Law, My Mom

You welcomed me before I married your daughter,
included me in family dinners, Santa Fe vacations,
gave me beautiful examples of how I should love.

Once we were married, you helped me learn to love
our children, family, friends, as my mother never did.
So many loving gestures filled your life, blessing mine.

That year you were dying, body ravaged by cancer,
in pain but not showing it, you were kind, loving,
glad to have me help take care of you on weekends.

Your final goodbye, the tone of your voice more than
what you said, let me know you were pleased I'd sit
with you that final night to look after your needs.

And that Sunday afternoon as you slipped slowly, softly
into death, not speaking, I felt so very blessed that you
would share your final, peaceful, sacred breath with me.

My Sense of Time Has Changed

As I went to school, became an adult,
time had always seemed to be cyclical,
hours ticked off by hands on a clock,

days, weeks, months on calendar pages,
and a new calendar hung as months
became a new year. Then it repeated.

Now time has gone down a rabbit hole,
entered a time warp, traveled through
a metaphorical doorway, become linear.

It's now a wave moving slowly across
an ocean toward a shore an unknown
distance off, an unmeasurable distance.

One day, probably soon, the shore will
suddenly be close. The wave will break
on shoals, disappear, a hiss in the sand.

Letter to a Woman I Met at a Writing Workshop

I doubt you recall that July night in '76 at Vedauwoo.
We sat in a school van in a thunderstorm and talked
about poetry and nature, watched the parking lot flood,
lightning reflect off the huge wet boulders, listened
to hollow, booming thunder. When the storm cleared,
the setting sun shone brightly under the clouds, painted
the boulders gold, curled a double rainbow over them.

The next day we went to Medicine Bow where we
found bright yellow flowers — neither knew their name —
learned later avalanche lilies. Those lilies, the creek
gurgling under a rock field, the upside down mountain
floating in the lake, the stunted krummholz clinging
to rocks at tree line, their roots like claws, their branches
flagged away from the wind, all excited you. Wonder
shone from your face, lit up your smile, your eyes.

You never knew that soon I'd learn the names of birds,
wildflowers, grasses, trees, share nature's wonders with
others. That I would discover Mary Oliver, Ted Kooser,
Maxine Kumin, not your poets, Cummings, Hopkins,
Wordsworth, but poets who helped me to love poetry.

Thank you for changing my life, pointing me to poetry,
introducing me to the joys of nature. You rescued me
from flashbacks of combat, guilt over men I'd killed,
their families shattered. Your child-like wonder and joy,
nudged me out of a rut I was in, led me into a new life
I never would have guessed could be mine.

Sincerely, and in eternal gratitude,
a man you met at a writing workshop.

> *Sadly, this letter will never be sent, for when I searched*
> *for her I found her obit. She had died three years before.*

How Time Has Weathered Me

As the pup and I turn to head home
on our walk, a bit sooner than usual,
I think about how the dog, now nine,
has aged recently, trouble with stairs,
turning sooner on walks, sleeping
more, I realize that I too have aged,
perhaps not as quickly or noticeably.
I've lived longer, aged more slowly.

In my twenties in college I fenced,
beat opponents because I'd learned
to use my speed and focus my mind
to anticipate an opponent's moves
and parry them. I then learned to fly,
training my mind and body, skills
that saved my life later in combat.

Then in my thirties and forties, I ran,
five, ten miles a day, twenty-six mile
marathons, using gifts I was blessed
with to build endurance and strength.

Now in my ninth decade, I don't run.
The pup and I saunter on our walks,
stop to smell the roses. We go a mile,
or a mile and a half, but never farther
than two. The pace not six and a half
minutes a mile, but twenty or more.
I don't fly except when writing poetry.

When I worry about my weathering,
I think of Monument Valley and how
wind and water have shaped arches,
the mittens, Shiprock, other red rocks.
How they sculpted the Black Canyon
of the Gunnison, the Grand Canyon.

At the Cardio Rehab Center

The physical therapist holds his right arm
as she gently helps him onto the treadmill.
She shows him how to set speed and stop,
points to a woman who'll monitor his heart
from a small black box strapped to his chest.

Today's the first day of rehab. It's been six
weeks since his triple-bypass and he's only
begun to regain his strength. He's walked
some, slowly, on sidewalks near his house.

He starts the treadmill and walks slowly.
Twinges of pain flicker through his chest.
He looks at the woman monitoring his heart
who looks back with a warm reassuring smile.
Ignoring the twinges, he continues to walk.

I Want My Forty-year-old Body Back

It could run marathons, had once run to
the top of 14-thousand foot Pikes Peak.
It ran five to ten miles almost every day,
didn't creak and pop the first few steps
in the morning as it got out of bed.

It could eat a full slab of barbecued ribs,
down them with two big glasses of beer,
and not put on an ounce. And it didn't
shy from the sizzle of the barbecue sauce
or yack it up in the middle of the night.

It could teach three classes during the day,
fly a five-hour mission that night, hauling
cadets to a meet and back the same day,
get up early next morning, mow the lawn,
and do several hours of yard work.

It could hike miles through mountains
to a good fishing stream, could climb
miles up a snowy mountain pass road
on cross-country skis, eat some lunch,
glide back down, and drive home.

Yes, that was a damn good body, one I'd
like to have back, as long as I didn't have
to make the same crazy mistakes I made
between 40 and 85. If I had to, I'd stick
with this creaky old wreck.

I Try to Calculate my Net Worth

I've seen in the media the net worth of politicians
and celebrities as though an indicator of success.
Net worth is defined as the total of what one owns,
one's assets, minus what one owes, one's debts.
So I thought I'd see what my net worth might be.

It would seem easy to add the value of the house —
can get that off the tax form--to the value of the car —
get that off the car registration form-- for a quick
approximation of what I own, my assets. And not
having any debts, that would be my net worth.
But I got to thinking about some not so visible
assets and debts I should own up to.

My parents raised me in tough times — the great
depression and then World War II — and from them
I've learned the value of integrity, honesty, courage.
How much is having good character worth?
How much do I owe my parents?

I've been very blessed with some great teachers,
from Mrs. Kenneth in first grade on through my
teachers in grade school, high school, college,
and graduate school. Then there's also Ed Sledge
who taught me to fly, and do it safely. Can I ever
put a value on what those teachers gave me?

Then there is the love that I've shared with my wife
and two kids. They taught me to love and be loved.
My parents didn't teach me. And that, Robert Frost
wrote, has made all the difference.

How can I ever repay these debts? It's obvious that
I owe much more than I can repay.

Faces from the Long-Ago Past

Sixty-five years ago, just over two hundred of us
graduated from the Academy and headed off
to pilot training or to navigate bombers, tankers,
and transports. We'd been together four years,
at times in the same squadrons, teams, classes,
and had gotten to know each other pretty well,
each name attached to a twenty-something face.

In the early years, we'd find out that one of us
had been killed in an aircraft accident and others
in Vietnam,. Then the long years after the war,
after we'd stopped flying, moved into new lives,
we slowed our dying. This last week I got emails
about three classmates who have flown west,
two from natural causes, one from cancer.

These last dozen years, all of us passing through
our eighties, some their nineties, notices of death
have come faster. The alumni quarterly often has
photos of gatherings and reunions of classmates
and I don't recognize them. So now when I hear
of a death, I see the face of a twenty-something,
not an old man closer to death than graduation.

About the Author

Art Elser is a poet and writer who has been published in many journals and anthologies. His books include a memoir, *What's It All About, Alfie?*, and seven books of poetry, *We Leave the Safety of the Sea, A Death at Tollgate Creek, As The Crow Flies, To See a World in a Grain of Sand, It Seemed Innocent Enough, A High Plains Year in Haiku,* and *It Begins in Silence, Ends in Grace*. Art lives in Denver with his wife, Kathy, and their pup, Lola.

www.ingramcontent.com/pod-product-compliance
Lightning Source LLC
Chambersburg PA
CBHW072219070526
44585CB00015B/1401